Figures & Figurations

ALSO BY OCTAVIO PAZ

Configurations

A Draft of Shadows

Eagle or Sun?

Early Poems 1935–1955

Selected Poems

Collected Poems 1957–1987

A Tree Within

Sunstone

A Tale of Two Gardens: Poems from India

OCTAVIO PAZ
MARIE JOSÉ PAZ
Figures & Figurations

TRANSLATED BY ELIOT WEINBERGER

AFTERWORD BY YVES BONNEFOY
Translated by Esther Allen

A NEW DIRECTIONS BOOK

Figures & Figurations was originally published in Spanish in 1999 by
Galaxia Gutenberg, S.A., and Círculo de Lectores (Barcelona)
as *Figuras y figurations*.

Design by Sylvia Frezzolini Severance
Manufactured in the United States of America
New Directions Books are printed on acid-free paper.
First published clothbound in 2002
Published simultaneously in Canada by Penguin Books Canada Ltd.

Library of Congress Cataloging-in-Publication Data

Paz, Octavio, 1914–
  [Figuras y figuraciones. English]
  Figures & figurations / Octavio Paz & Marie José Paz ; translated by
Eliot Weinberger ; afterword by Yves Bonnefoy ; translated by Esther Allen.
    p. cm.
  ISBN 0-8112-1524-5 (cloth : alk. paper)
  I. Title: Figures and figurations. II. Paz, Marie José.
  III. Weinberger, Eliot. IV. Title.
  PQ7297.P285 F5413 2002
  861'.62—dc21   2002008697

New Directions Books are published for James Laughlin
by New Directions Publishing Corporation,
80 Eighth Avenue, New York, NY 10011

CONTENTS

I

II

III

I

CALM

Sand-clock moon:
night empties out,
the hour is lit.

Calma

[Calm, 1994]

YOUR FACE

A hand—whose hand?—
blue skin, red nails,
holding a palette.
I want to be a face, says the palette.
And the hand turns it into a mirror,
and in the mirror, your eyes,
and your eyes become trees, hills, clouds.
A path winds through the double row
of insinuations and allusions.
On this path I reach your mouth,
fountain of truths just born.

La paleta

[Palette, 1992]

THE BRUSHES AWAKE

Creature of wind, whirlwind of whitecaps,
a dragon between floating clouds
and a ball of fire spinning
in a sky that looks like earth.

Little dragon, you lope
through a dream of sleeping brushes,
barely a puff of air
that half-opens eyelids.

The box unfolds its wings and begins to fly.

La boîte aux nuages

[Cloud Box, 1991]

IMPERIAL FIREPLACE

Flames have turned to stone
and the stones a group of pyramids,
quiet geometry beneath an unmarked sky.

Two sphinx-paws defend it,
two recumbent lions watch over,
guarding the portico,
two other lions, winged, dressed
in the aquatic arms of the Nile.
A double emblem of desert and water,
sterile powers
that joined, procreate.

Little monument of fire
in a corner of the room.
Egypt burning,
encrusted on the façade of winter.

La chemineé empire

[Imperial Fireplace, 1989]

CIPHER

Wall tattooed with signs
like the body of the starry night.
Up there, neither clouds nor stars:
an architecture of wood,
arcades and niches populated by echoes.

Horizon of petrified time:
each stamp is a cipher,
each cipher a window,
each window a glance
that drills through the days
and unveils its face:
not of yesterday or tomorrow, but of now.

The windows are stamps
and the stamps are omens
turned into fortunes:
The couple meets and entwines.
She and he are a living stamp,
the undressed cipher of the daily beginning again.

Le sceau

[Seal, 1991]

INDIA

These letters and sinuous lines
that entwine and separate on the paper
are like the palm of a hand:
are they India?
          And the paw of tawny metal
—forged by the sun, chilled by the moon—
its claws squeezing a hard glass ball
and the iridescent sphere,
the thousands of candles, burning and shining,
that the faithful launch each night,
floating on the lakes and rivers:
are they a prophecy, a riddle,
the memory of an encounter,
the scattered signs of fortune?

—They are the scepter of chance,
left at the foot of the tree of time
by the king of this world.

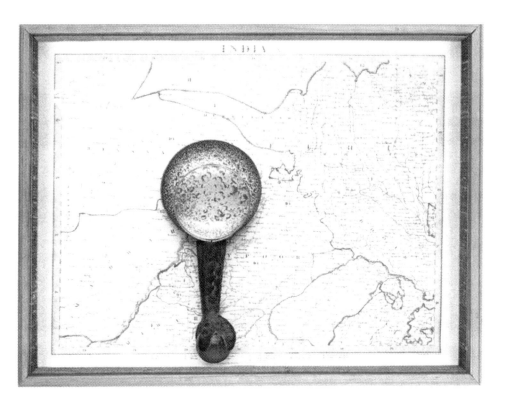

India

[1991]

Enigma

We are born from a question,
each one of our acts
is a question,
our years are a forest of questions,
you are a question and I am another,
God is the hand that tirelessly writes
universes in the form of questions.

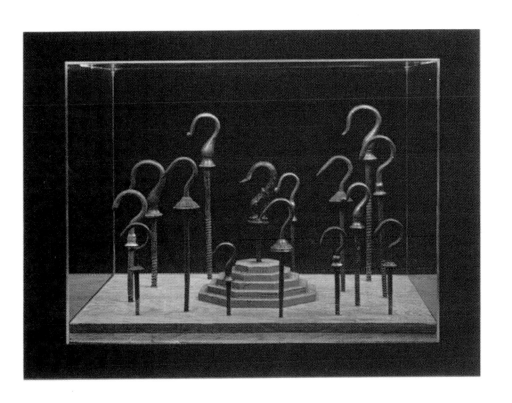

La forêt s'interroge

[The Forest Asks Itself, 1992]

DOOR

What's behind that door?
Don't knock, don't ask, no one answers,
nothing can open it,
not the picklock of curiosity
nor the little key of reason,
nor the hammer of impatience.
Don't talk, don't ask,
come closer, put your ear to it,
can't you hear it breathing?
There, on the other side,
someone like you asks:
what's behind that door?

Puerta

[Door, 1994]

THE ARMS OF THE TRADE

Coat of arms: two knitting needles,
swords crossed over an emblem,
brocade the color of ivory and a grayish blue.
Shield: a mother-of-pearl miniature
turned into a spool of white thread.

Two satin cushions,
heart and memory,
stuck with tiny pins:
worries, feelings, desires, joys,
solitudes, farewells, encounters,
that which time gives us and takes away,
the moment palpable and forever evanescent,
time that moves at a tortoise's pace
or a sudden flash:
if you touch it, it escapes, it returns when you forget it.

Other spools of multicolored thread
to sew memories and forebodings,
the lunges and cringes of life.

Two hands, diligent embroiderers
of the cloth that covers and undresses,
waving like a flag, floating like perfume,
an armor made of air
for the battle of two bodies.

Les armes du métier

[The Arms of the Trade, 1990]

THE CONSTELLATION OF THE BODY

Eyes born of night
are not eyes that see:
they are eyes that invent
what we see.

Theater of metamorphosis:
in the center of time
the rotation of the heavens
has stopped for a moment,
as long as the glance that sees it.

The stars are seeds,
sprouting in the subheavens.

Time plays chess with its shadow;
mirror that unfolds in reflections,
reflections that disappear:
the winner loses, the loser wins.

In the lens of his kaleidoscope
the astronomer sees the constellation
turned into a woman, a wave of clarity.

It is the dawn that returns to earth:
closing the eyes of night,
it opens the eyes of men.

Les yeux de la nuit

[The Eyes of the Night, 1992]

The Dream of Pens

The blue hand
has become a sketch pen.
Above, Mt. Fuji is born,
dressed in white.
Slope of tall grasses:
three pines and a ghost.
Some swallows ask for the moon.
Below, on a bed of worn velvet,
steel pens sleep.
They are seeds that dream of their resurrection:
tomorrow they will be fountains.

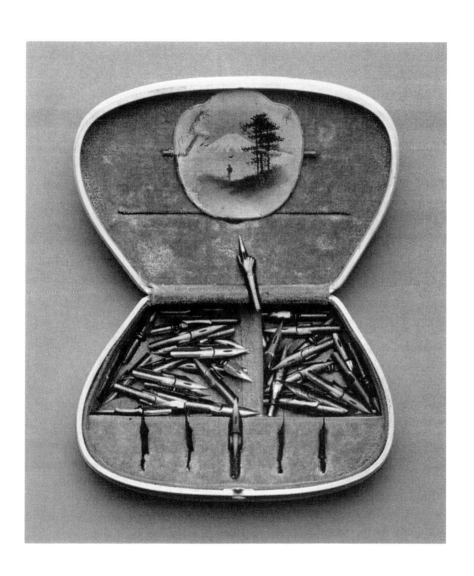

La plume bleue

[The Blue Pen, 1991]

HERE

My steps in this street
echo
     in another street
where
     I hear my steps
stepping in this street
where
only the mist is real

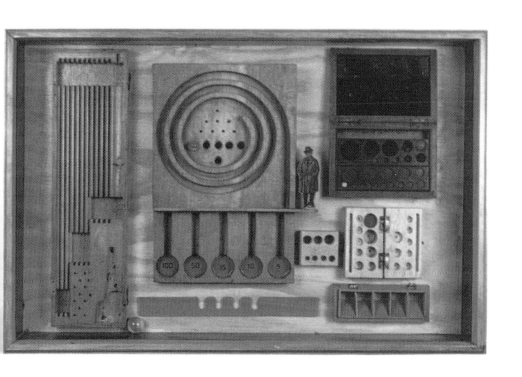

Aquí

[Here, 1994]

II

CALMA

Luna, reloj de arena:
la noche se vacía
la hora se ilumina.

from Árbol adentro / A Tree Within, *1987*

Tu rostro

Una mano—¿de quién?—
la piel azul, las uñas rojas,
sostiene una paleta.
Quiero ser cara, dice la paleta.
Y la mano la convierte en espejo
y en el espejo aparecen tus ojos
y tus ojos se vuelven árboles, nubes, colinas.
Un sendero serpea entre la doble hilera
de las insinuaciones y las alusiones.
Por ese sendero llego a tu boca,
fuente de verdades recién nacidas.

Houston, July 23, 1994

LOS PINCELES DESPIERTAN

Criatura de viento, remolino de espuma,
un dragón entre nubes flotantes
y una bola de fuego rodando
en un cielo parecido a la tierra.

Dragoncillo, tú trotas
en un sueño de pinceles dormidos
y eres un soplo apenas
que entreabre sus párpados.

La caja abre las alas y comienza a volar.

Mexico City, September 23, 1994

LA CHIMENEA IMPERIO

Las llamas se volvieron piedras
y las piedras una asamblea de pirámides,
quieta geometría bajo un cielo sin tacha.

La defienden dos zarpas de esfinges,
la velan dos leones sedentes,
hacen guardia en el pórtico
otros dos leones alados, revestidos
con las armas acuáticas del Nilo.
Doble emblema del desierto y del agua,
las potencias estériles
que al juntarse procrean.

Pequeño monumento de fuego
en un ángulo del salón.
Egipto incandescente
incrustado en la frente del invierno.

Mexico City, September 27, 1994

CIFRA

Muro tatuado de signos
como el cuerpo de la noche estrellada.
Arriba, ni nubes ni astros:
una arquitectura de madera,
arcadas, oquedades pobladas de ecos.

Horizonte de tiempo petrificado:
cada sello es una cifra,
cada cifra una ventana,
cada ventana una mirada
que perfora los días
y desvela su rostro:
no el de ayer o mañana, el de ahora

Las ventanas son sellos
y los sellos son signos
resueltos en sinos:
la pareja se encuentra y se enlaza.
Ella y él son el sello viviente,
la desnudada cifra del diario recomienzo.

Mexico City, October 7, 1994

INDIA

Estas letras y líneas sinuosas
que en el papel se enlazan y separan
como sobre la palma de una mano:
¿son la India?
                    Y la pata de metal leonado
—forjado por el sol, enfriado por la luna—
su garra que oprime una dura bola de vidrio
y la esfera iridiscente
donde arden y brillan los millares de velas
que, cada noche, los devotos
lanzan a navegar por lagos y por ríos:
¿son una profecía, un acertijo,
la memoria de un encuentro,
los signos dispersos de un destino?

—Son el cetro del azar.
Lo dejó, al pie del árbol del tiempo,
el rey de este mundo.

Mexico City, October 9, 1994

34

ENIGMA

Nacimos de una pregunta,
cada uno de nuestros actos
es una pregunta,
nuestros años son un bosque de preguntas,
tú eres una pregunta y yo soy otra,
Dios es una mano que dibuja, incansable,
universos en forma de preguntas.

New York, July 14, 1994

PUERTA

¿Qué hay detrás de esa puerta?
No llames, no preguntes, nadie responde,
nada puede abrirla,
ni la ganzúa de la curiosidad
ni la llavecita de la razón
ni el martillo de la impaciencia.
No hables, no preguntes,
acércate, pega la oreja:
¿no oyes una respiración?
Allá del otro lado,
alguien como tú pregunta:
¿qué hay detrás de esa puerta?

Mexico City, September 26, 1994

Las armas del oficio

Blasón: dos agujas de gancho,
espadas cruzadas sobre un emblema,
un brocado color marfil y azul grisáceo.
Escudo: una miniatura de nácar
vuelta un carrete de hilo blanco.

Dos almohadillas de raso,
el corazón y la memoria,
atravesados por alfileres diminutos:
penas, corazonadas, deseos, alegrías,
soledades, despedidas, encuentros,
lo que el tiempo nos da y lo que nos quita,
el instante palpable y siempre evanescente,
el tiempo que anda a paso de tortuga
o es súbita centella:
si lo tocas, se fuga, regresa si lo olvidas.

Otros carretes de hilos multicolores
para coser recuerdos y presentimientos,
saltos y sobresaltos de la vida.

Dos manos, aplicadas bordadoras
de la tela que cubre y que desnuda,
ondea como bandera, flota como perfume,
armadura hecha de aire
para el combate de dos cuerpos.

Mexico City, September 27, 1994

Constelación corporal

Los ojos nacidos de la noche
no son ojos que miran:
son ojos que inventan
lo que nosotros miramos.

Teatro de las metamorfosis:
en el centro de la hora
la rotación del cielo
se ha detenido por un instante,
largo como la mirada que la mira.

La estrellas son semillas
y germinan en los subcielos.

El tiempo juega al ajedrez con su sombra;
espejo que se desdobla en reflejos,
reflejos que se desvanecen:
el que gana, pierde y el que pierde, gana.

En la lente de su caleidoscopio
el astrónomo mira a la constelación
convertida en mujer, ola de claridad.

Es el alba qu vuelve a la tierra:
al cerrar los ojos de la noche
abre los ojos de los hombres.

Mexico City, October 14, 1994

Sueño de plumas

La mano azul
se ha vuelto pluma dibujante.
Arriba nace el Fuji,
vestido de blanco.
Ladera de yerbas altas:
brotan tres pinos y un fantasma.
Unas golondrinas preguntan por la luna.
Abajo, en un lecho de terciopelo ajado,
duermen plumas aceradas.
Son semillas que sueñan su resurrección:
mañana serán surtidores.

Paris, May 1991

AQUÍ

Mis pasos en esta calle
resuenan
       en otra calle
donde
     oigo mis pasos
pasar en esta calle
donde
sólo es real la niebla

from Salamandra / Salamander, *1962*

III

THE WHITECAPS OF THE HOURS

For more than fifteen years I have been a witness to a passion-
ate and secret project. Marie José collects all kinds of little
objects and bits of rubbish, papers of various colors and tex-
tures, ribbons, postage stamps, buttons, clasps, pins, old
engravings, photographs (sometimes taken by herself: an inch
of asphalt, a puddle and its archipelago of bubbles, a piece of
paper as crumpled as the Sierra Madre), illustrations from
books and magazines, labels, tickets, theater programs, matches,
wrappers—the treasures and detritus that the wave of time
abandons every day. The whitecaps of the hours. . . Marie José
cuts and recuts, glues and unglues, scrapes and polishes, paints
and repaints, makes and unmakes and remakes until all of these
pieces are gathered on a stiff board and, drawn by the magnet
of her imagination, form configurations of colors and rhythms.
Some are crystallizations of translucent substances floating in
memory and others are solidifications of light, wind, thought.

A flora of needles, vegetations ruled by a triangle's obses-
sion and the eccentricity of an ellipse; optical pyramids; sky-
scrapers of chromatic aberrations; crossroads of perspectives; a
universe made from a drop of water and a drop of ink; mirrors
where glances sail and reason gets lost; immense deserts on an
inch of celluloid; gardens of telephones; green, yellow, and blue
stamps; cellophane gnomes with Roman numeral buttons; tra-
pezes of thread and skeins of transparencies; princes and
princesses of brown paper; ballerina propellers; sarabandes of

reflections, echoes, forms; metal discs with wings: dragonflies! Animated objects that, without saying a word, speak to us in unknown languages that we almost understand.

Vocation begins with a calling. It is an awakening of the faculties and the inclinations that have been sleeping within us and which, summoned by a voice that comes from somewhere we don't know, wake us and reveal to us a part of our inner lives. Discovering our vocations we discover ourselves; it is a second birth. For that reason, many artists change their names from the one given by their parents to the one given by their vocation. The new name is a sign or, more exactly, a countersign that opens the way to a hidden region of themselves. Vocation comes from *vocatio*, calling; *vocatio* in turn comes from *vox*.

The word originally meant, according to the *Dictionary of Authorities*, "the inspiration with which God calls to a state of perfection, especially in that of religion." God has many different ways of calling and, in the Bible, many of them are mute: silent signals, signals that we must decipher.

Although the religious significance of vocation has been extended to other fields, primarily to art and thought, the word entails, in all cases, two correlated acts: the call and the answer. Who or what calls us? We never know with any certainty: it is an exterior agent, a force, an event of apparent insignificance but charged with meaning, a word heard by chance—who knows? Nevertheless, although it comes from outside, it becomes part of ourselves. The vocation is the calling that, on one day unlike all the others, is given us and to which we cannot help but respond, if we want to truly be. The calling obliges us to leave ourselves. Vocation is a bridge that takes us to other worlds that are our true world.

Marie José's vocation was born one afternoon in the fall of 1971 in New York. Joseph Cornell, having heard from a mutual friend, Dore Ashton, that we wanted to meet him, invited us to his house. We had corresponded some years before, when Marie José and I were living in India and he had been given a prize for sculpture at the first Delhi Biennial. Dore and her daughter went with us, and we arrived at around five in the afternoon. Cornell lived in Queens, on Utopia Parkway, a long street and anonymous, as though it were proving the banality of all utopias. A small house of unpainted wood, a wilted lawn, three steps, and a door. We knocked. Cornell himself answered. White-haired, slightly bent over, slow in words and gestures. He was wearing a dark gray suit and a white shirt without a tie. A long and bony face, pronounced features, deep and melancholic eyes—what color were they?—reserve, irony, a certain eccentricity, and an air of having coming from the other side of reality.

We walked through a little room of nondescript furniture and a tarnished mirror between two faded photographs, along a creaky hallway with a cupboard crammed with books and boxes, and went down a steep staircase to the basement. It was his studio. Two or three spacious rooms like Ali Baba's cave, and like it, full of treasures. With polite and timid gestures, Cornell showed us a few fragile and marvelous constructions. He seemed astonished that they were his own work. Stalactites formed not by water but by time— by time transmuted into visions. Marie José was fascinated: it was though she *recognized* those objects.

They recognized each other. Cornell was also fascinated by Marie José: the charm was reciprocal. Did he see in her a reincarnation of Carlotta Grissi or a skater escaped from a story

45

by Selma Lagerlöf? And did she see in him an ancient wizard capable of resuscitating the best part of childhood: the faculty of wonder? I don't know. But I do know that, that afternoon, she saw her vocation.

We returned to Cambridge, where we were then living. Not long after, Marie José received an envelope that contained a mysterious message. A joke from Cornell. She replied with another. There was a brief exchange of signs, countersigns, and enigmas, interrupted by our return to Mexico City, and then ended by Cornell's death in 1972. We went back to Cambridge, to another apartment. Marie José began to make collages, assemblages, and "poetic constructions," as Miró had called his three-dimensional objects. A few friends saw these pieces, among them Roman Jakobson. As is well known, he was interested in the visual arts and more than once he noted the affinities between his phonological theory and Cubism: in each case, it deals with a system of relations, in the former among phonemes and in the latter among lines, forms, and volumes. Marie José's collages immediately captivated him because he saw in them the same principle of associations and correspondences among apparently different objects. It is the cardinal principle of the arts, particularly of poetry, but it vitalizes all systems.

For the Stoics, the universe was a system, that is, a conjunction of distinct elements that form an organic whole. In that sense, one might say that a poem, a sonata, or a painting are systems like the solar, respiratory, nervous, or molecular systems. Jakobson was right: each one of Marie José's collages is a metaphor, and the most realized among them are small self-contained universes, true systems of visual and poetic relations. Jakobson's enthusiasm persuaded her to keep working.

Elizabeth Bishop was another witness of these first attempts. Her eye was keen, the vision of a poet and of a painter. She felt a strange but not inexplicable affinity for artists such as Schwitters, the grand master of collage. Elizabeth was immediately attracted to Marie José's compositions, ruled by psychic forces analogous to those of her poems: fragments and stray particles that the magnet of her imagination collected, arranged, and transformed into objects given their own lives.

There is another word I would like to mention: sympathy. It was how the Stoics designated the universal forces of attraction that unite elements and beings. Sympathy: cosmic friendship. . . A few other friends—Mark Strand and Robert Gardner, among them—also encouraged her. Nevertheless, despite their insistence (and mine), for many years she refused to exhibit her work. Now, finally, she has agreed to do so, and I write these lines to celebrate her decision.

Marie José's collages and assemblages, all of them small, made from the fragile materials that chance and desire have presented to her, are the extraordinary results of work and of play. The two activities are contradictory: play redeems work and work gives dignity to play. The variety of styles, subjects, and techniques is natural in work that has been realized over a period of more than fifteen years. Despite their diversity, the surprising thing about them is their unity. Not a unity of concept but rather of sensibility and vision. These two words define her work: sensibility is sensation, instinct, emotion; vision is sensation given form, emotion transformed into objects that we simultaneously perceive with our senses and with our minds.

The ancients used the word "fantasy" to designate that

faculty which turns sensations into forms; the moderns call it "imagination." The central aspect of this faculty is its aptitude to discover the relations between things and thus to invent or create new objects. The art of Marie José is an example of this faculty: she combines dissimilar forms and elements, discovers the hidden relations among them, and unites them in a visual concert that does not exclude oppositions, asymmetries, and humor. She transforms sensations into vision, and vision into a living object. These objects sometimes surprise us and some-times make us dream or laugh (humor is one of the poles of her work). Signs that invite us on a motionless voyage of fan-tasy, bridges to the infinitely small or to galactic distances, windows that open on a nowhere. Marie José's art is a dialogue between here and there.

Configurations of forms and colors on an unmoving board: their silence is a pause, in the manner of a butterfly that rests for a moment on a dizzying flower. A world in motion— toward where? Skyscrapers that burn and die out, stairways that rise and vanish above or descend and are transformed into tunnels of echoes that are lost in the silence, stairways going up or down—toward where? Compasses, sails, boats, globes beneath stopped watches and arrested suns—toward where? Skaters that glide over a rink of ellipses, tightrope walkers bal-anced on the horizon line, a dance of reflections, birds, arrows, kites, comets—toward where? Creatures and forms that walk, fly, swim, and rock suspended between silence and motion, daughters of vertigo—toward where? Signs that trace an inquiry and hesitate between staying here and leaving for there. But where is here and where is there?

OCTAVIO PAZ

Mexico City, 1990

AFTERWORD:

OCTAVIO AND MARIE JOSÉ

Octavio Paz and Marie José: from the day they met, their friends could not imagine one without the other. Life did not give the lie to that impression of a complementarity as intense as it was happy; life's external laws have only broken what came into being in accordance with its other, secret will. Now that this little book which Octavio and Marie José conceived, planned, and carried out together is given to us, the memories flow, more than thirty years of memories, and the continual example of a union of two people who were profoundly occupied with each other and yet open to friendships and great causes, their very deep seriousness mingled with movement and laughter. Anyone who has known and loved those two cannot look at these pages and read these words without thinking immediately of the artist and the poet who willed them into being.

Yet these images and poems also have a life of their own that transcends the circumstances of their birth, and the book's words and pictures soon compel the interest even of those who at first think of their creators; this is not to suggest one approach over another, but to reveal that the relationship between the woman who created these collages and the man who commented upon them could evolve into a general reflection upon things while at the same time remaining an event in the life they shared. Why? Because two minds came together in this book to think about what poetry is, in and of itself, and about what collage is; to perceive the intuitions inherent in these two practices and their sometimes divergent temptations, but also to investigate how they might rediscover, support, and reaffirm each other. The bond between Octavio and Marie José only affords us a greater awareness of what is at play in the work of signs, work that varies from one field to another but is illuminated by juxtaposition.

As it happens, the initial concern of both poetry and collage is the fact of dissociation and the desire for unity, in other words, that element of a sign (whether the sign be a word or an artist's creation) which turns away from immediate perception by viewing the world from particular angles and therefore fragmenting it infinitely, while at the same time remembering the great unravaged reality thus effaced and forgotten, and sometimes seeking to return to it. That movement of return is poetry. Through their rhythms and images, poems attempt, specifically and fundamentally, to rediscover, in the words they use and restore to dignity, the full presence of things and, through that presence, a unity in the visible reality of the world and of life, which the person writing or reading the poem feels, perhaps illusorily, on the verge of participating in, to the greater harmony of his relations with himself and others. Within language, poetry is the movement of systole, which reassembles the world that, for us, is scattered by all the words that substitute for empirical reality.

But when the poetical act thus reassembles, it reassembles in the very place—the word—where the fragmentation occurs; and this fact inevitably establishes that the poem, even as it sets out to transgress against ordinary meaning (which remains outside, trapped in the snare of conceptual thought), will nevertheless contain the obstacle of that meaning, its endless resistance. And the poet, the apprentice poet, does not cease to struggle with this, though he must understand all the while that this constraint also fascinates him. Might that not be because the transgression he wishes to commit has no chance of becoming real unless it takes place within the very heart of what it seeks to transgress against? If it were to forget the great conceptual current that crosses every word, poetry would be mere utopia, a discourse upon itself, and not true action. The greatest poets are aware of this danger, which ensures the fundamentally dialectic nature of their work.

And collage? Collage would seem to go directly against poetry's goal of reassembly in a place beyond the region of the spirit where signifieds construct and deconstruct their always abstract and partial representation of what is. To tear apart an image —painting or photography—in order to place one fragment of it next to a strip torn from another image, to remove an object from its habitual environment in order to implicate it within an unforeseen and irrational relationship with other objects in another context (the initial fragment stripped, at least apparently, of all sense) is certainly, on first sight, to do away with the coherent reading of things that institutes and reassures the authority of the concept—the level of language which poetry also refuses. But in collage that refusal is of a different order, for collage does not erase from the signs, figures, and forms it employs that which keeps them within the level of language most simply concerned with its own everyday interests and points of view. On this bit of newspaper pasted alongside a label torn from a bottle or a packet of cigarettes certain phrases remain and continue speaking of an event and evoking the ideas that went with it, and while these references no longer count as such at that level of our attention, they nevertheless preserve language's mass of signifiers and signifieds, like a vast substance which remains the horizon of the movement that takes place. Collage, then, transgresses against the aims and devices of the discourse of words by remaining within the space of that discourse. Rather than denying their vocation for significance, it seeks to give new meanings to that space's signifiers, undermining readings but only in order to instill a desire to invent other, truer, and more complex readings that go farther in their conception and interpretation of the world's perpetual becoming. In short, collage is, or very much seems to be, still on the side of language and not on that of the immediacy of sensory experience, with which language has no acquaintance.

Might not collage, from this specific perspective, be a decentering, a subversion, a breaking down of the orthodoxies of the word in order to attempt other forms of knowledge?—though always at the level of thought, which defines and analyzes. Diastole itself: the decomposition of the immediate, encouraged and accelerated by the working mind's own critique of the insufficient conceptions of science and the snares and lies of social existence, a critique which thus forges ahead with its deconstructions and reconstructions of a reality reduced to the formulae that are projected onto it. Mediation—which in the everyday practice of the world is hyperactivated and taken for the sole locus of truth.

If so, or if always so, this is the exact opposite of poetry's ambition. And in Octavio and Marie José Paz's book we therefore confront two contradictory operations, as well as a comparison between them which arose very naturally out of reciprocal affection within two shared lives. With perhaps also, on the part of the poet, the desire to observe, under a different guise from the one he perceives in the poem—the poem as it exists—that fatality of meaning which is opposed to the witnessing of presence and, in the poet's work as in the collages, takes on the form of concepts which, when disrupted, can do nothing except transform, but without renouncing their status as ideas, thought, object producers: without returning to the simplicity of the world. Events in the writing of fact, which make the search for unity another contribution, indirect, perhaps, but intense, to the necessary (particularly in today's society) questioning of the orthodoxies of the intellect and morality.

However, I will note here that Marie José Paz's beautiful collages have, in their immediate appearance, at least as much unity (and thus as much harmony) as is implied beneath their appeals for a subversion of the means and forms of the orthodoxies of thought and the ways of being and feeling those orthodoxies encourage. Upon this critical aim, supposedly the specific vocation of collage, they superimpose a spatial organization that creates a site where fragmentations and displacements of fragments inscribe a reality for themselves, a plastic reality, whose power of composition (which is to say of reassembly, passage beyond the need to analyze, silence) is its essential manifestation, its teaching. Here, at one level of the work, is what decenters, what breaks down, and the endless metamorphosis of concepts into other concepts continues; but here, as well, now on a higher level, is what unifies, with an authority that overrides the disruption and displacement—

this cutting and pasting in order to startle—which are the fundamental characteristics of an art that was invented, let us not forget, both by the two musicians who were Picasso and Braque during the Cubist period, and by the terrorists of language, of whom Schwitters remains the great example. Are Marie José Paz's collages dedicated to language in order to precipitate it into its becoming, in juxtaposition with the poems which, in their turn, seek moments of presence that will transfigure the word? And are they not also, just as much if not more, that which goes beyond the charming hustle and bustle of concepts in order to show, by means of form—the nonverbal, transverbal rapport of forms—that life is worth living only when the lesson of the immediate restructures and makes music of the disorder of the intellect as it labors on the construction sites of a more external knowledge?

This is what I see in them, at any rate, and I would say, in a word, that they listen to the poetry and understand the poetry's wants just as, for his part, Octavio Paz, in this book, gazes upon and considers and takes entirely seriously the dual intuition which collage can evince. These works, each of them grave and resonant, respond to poetry's desire by telling it that while their quest most assuredly favors and seems even to extol decentering, deferral, and subversion in the economy of signs, those who consecrate themselves to this quest are aware of what they risk losing, but can also understand that they are not without the power to speak that risk and repair that loss, bending the multiple towards the One, returning the word, which wanders among the chance encounters between systems of signs, to the silence born from the harmony between forms.

These collages, then, and this is not the least important

thing, allow the affinities hidden beneath the hasty figures that thought substitutes for things—a substitution cutting and pasting cannot undo—to reveal themselves and unfold beyond the initial moment of superficial surprise. And since the symbol, forewarned as it is of the finite nature of things, is more internal to life than the concept, these affinities, unearthed, meditated upon, and understood, will lead to a rediscovery of the lineaments of an architecture that makes possible a being-in-the-world returned to its simplest needs, those nourished by the sole fact of being recognized. A form for existence, which is so easily blinded and lost. A crystallization within the spirit, as Octavio says in his commentary on the collages. Diastole and systole reunited, a work that throbs like a heart.

Among these affinities is this one, which may be the great key, as well as a contribution that could not be more natural and direct and almost specific to the art of collage when it becomes aware of the two levels of its powerful truth: On the one hand, collage has the capacity to indicate the direction and meaning of timelessness, by the harmony of form embodied in its crumbling figures. Yet on the other hand it is also a fact, and perhaps a more fundamental fact, that as we look at these cutouts—often worked in timeworn paper whose colors have faded or are about to fade—and at the delicate masonry that joins them, the artist and we with her are summoned to an awareness of the precariousness of this construction material and its subjugation to destructive time: the foundation of clay on which thought is erected. Timelessness and precariousness—certainly, at first glance, two very divergent affirmations. But don't we know, sometimes, that timelessness is an illusion only when we forget, in order to believe in that illusion, the work of time in our lives, the weight of its limits and its finitude upon us? Don't we know that only by devoting ourselves with glad hearts to the devastating reality of duration, perceiving the true conditions of life but also its powers, will we accede to instants of consciousness beyond the time of clocks: instants that will be the only timelessness of any value? There is an essential affinity between the absolute and the instant, each drinks from the other's wellspring, and the brittle paper of a collage offers to carry form beyond itself and into the invisible. That is what these images, in whispering but lucid voices, taught Marie Jo and Octavio Paz when they bent down to contemplate them together.

YVES BONNEFOY